# Wine Them, Dine Them, and Deny Them

## Tools to a progressive relationship

**DEACON FROST AND RIP MATHEWS**

BALBOA.PRESS
A DIVISION OF HAY HOUSE

Balboa Press books may be ordered through booksellers or by contacting:

Balboa Press
A Division of Hay House
1663 Liberty Drive
Bloomington, IN 47403
www.balboapress.com
844-682-1282

Because of the dynamic nature of the Internet, any web addresses or links contained in this book may have changed since publication and may no longer be valid. The views expressed in this work are solely those of the author and do not necessarily reflect the views of the publisher, and the publisher hereby disclaims any responsibility for them.

The author of this book does not dispense medical advice or prescribe the use of any technique as a form of treatment for physical, emotional, or medical problems without the advice of a physician, either directly or indirectly. The intent of the author is only to offer information of a general nature to help you in your quest for emotional and spiritual well-being. In the event you use any of the information in this book for yourself, which is your constitutional right, the author and the publisher assume no responsibility for your actions.

Any people depicted in stock imagery provided by Getty Images are models, and such images are being used for illustrative purposes only. Certain stock imagery © Getty Images.

Print information available on the last page.

ISBN: 979-8-7652-3013-8 (sc)
ISBN: 979-8-7652-3014-5 (e)

Balboa Press rev. date: 06/23/2022

# CONTENTS

Introduction ............................................................. ix

Self-Survey ............................................................ xiii

Important! ............................................................... xv

Chapter 1    You're Not the Problem; They Are ........ 1

Chapter 2    Establishing the Baseline ....................... 5
             *Case Study 1 Sergeant Jacobs* ..................... 9

Chapter 3    Making the Process Work for You ........ 11

Chapter 4    Keep the Faith ..................................... 17
             *Case Study 2 Kevin* ............................... 21

Chapter 5    Rinse and Repeat ................................. 25
             *Case Study 3 Firefighter Thomas* ............. 29

Cliffs Notes ............................................................ 31

Additional Key Terminology ................................. 33

About The Author .................................................. 35

I want to thank God for giving me the insight
to put these patterns together to help others.

# INTRODUCTION

Are you looking to save your relationship? Have you and your sweetheart recently split up? Does your world feel as if it is falling apart? Would you sacrifice anything to win them back? Then this is not the fucking book for you. If you're looking for another psychology book, then go look down the aisle of Barnes & Noble. This is simply a guideline on how to get your balls back (or ladies' balls) and how to take control of your life again.

Before we get started, I should chime in that we are in no shape or form a psychologist. Nor have we ever claimed to be. Nor do we ever attend on getting that license. We are simply two dudes who had failed relationships with multiple women. We have learned from patterns of our defeats, which developed into the concepts listed in this book.

In each of the chapters, we will build upon each concept and apply them to real relationships chaos. Yes, each of the examples provided is real. We did not make up any of them. Yes, we know that some of them are fucked up and you will be shaking your head back and forth. But don't worry, Dr. Phil. You can relax; we are not going to take over your show. But an invite would be nice.

So take this with a grain of salt, or don't. There is no easy way to regain control over your life. It is a long road where patience is a virtue you will actually need. Nothing changes over night. If you want change, then you are going to have to discipline. You are going to be constantly questioning yourself. Possibly ponder punching yourself in the balls. But that would be unsettling, so don't do that.

We do, however, promise that if you apply these concepts, you will see change in your relationship, or at least get your balls back. So I suggest you sit back, order yourself a pint of beer, maybe a shot or two of Jamo, and indulge yourself.

# SELF-SURVEY

Yes, we have a self-survey for you to take. Trust us: it's really simple. If you answer no, then this book is for you! We will help you change these answers! If you answer yes, then you should still read this book!

You will gain a better understanding of the human mind but from two cool dudes who actually experienced shit and didn't just read a psychology book. I mean really, how can you explain human behavior without fucking shit up with great friends and shitty relationships?

1. Are you sexually active? (With your partner or somebody else?)

2. Do you run the household in your relationship?

3. Can you live without sex in order to get what you want?

4. Have you been denied sex? If yes, why and how long? (Yes, we changed the rules on the last question.)

# IMPORTANT!

## Actual Case Studies

In case you were thinking we were full of shit, we have case studies that show the good and the bad of our method. As you will read, you will notice that some of the test subjects succeeded in their conquest while others failed. We will be pointing out where they went wrong so you can see how to succeed.

CHAPTER

1

# You're Not the Problem; They Are

If you decided to continue to read this and haven't gotten discouraged, then I would like to congratulate you on taking the first step toward becoming an alpha again. In most cases, we tend to commit to relationships that are destined to fail or cause more of a headache. We get comfortable with our current situation. Most times, we justify in our minds, *Well, fuck it. I don't want to start over and meet someone else.* This in turn causes many of us to have midlife crises rather than enjoy healthy relationships.

Most people prefer to continue to live how they are used to rather than shaking up the current dynamic. By doing this, we allow our partners to take advantage of our relationships. They tend to gain all the rewards, while you continue to be physically, mentally, and sexually frustrated.

In most cases, if you do not do the task that your significant other asks of you, then your partner will deny you of what you desire, whether it's sexual or an emotional boost. But let's bounce this idea out there. What if you turned the table on them and denied them of what you desired? Would that change their actions toward you?

The answer to that simple question is yes. Your partner feeds off your confidence. At some point in your relationship, they desired you because of your confidence and the security you provided. However, like in all relationships, disagreements and arguments occurred. This put tension on the relationship. Rather than standing up for yourself, you choose to fold this way. They aren't pissed off anymore. This way, you don't have to go to sleep with a headache. Sound familiar? The old cliché is "A happy wife, a happy life." Your norm continued, allowing you to go about your day.

However, little did you realize you began to give up control over your relationship. All relationships require an equal balance of control. Each individual wants their feelings and desires to be heard. When this is threatened, we become defensive and attack the other partner. Similar to a wild animal. We say things that will mentally bring down our partner. We know their ticks.

Realizing this is your first step to your recovery. In order for us to salvage any form of a relationship, we must acknowledge the fact that you didn't just fuck everything up. You are not 100 percent to blame. Yes, your partner might make you feel as if it's completely your fault. However, they do this to manipulate the situation to their benefit. They know you will eventually break and give them what they desire.

Now that this has been established, realize that you have complete control over your life. That's the first fucking step. You have the power to decide how others perceive you and how they respond to you. Before we take any other steps, you must rebuild your confidence, not just physically but mentally as well. Without being mentally strong, before continuing this process, you will fail in regaining your relationship.

Your partner will continue to challenge you when you aren't giving in as easily. She will act distant and cold, trying to make you chase them. However, you are stronger than that. She is now seeing the real you. Don't fucking forget that.

# CHAPTER

## Establishing the Baseline

Before we dive right into this exciting chapter, if you're easily offended, then you need to stop reading. This shit we're about to share is not easy to hear. If you heard what we were talking about in a bar, I'm sure the faint of heart would be offended. But the truth in order to regain control and respect in any relationship, you must establish your baseline.

Take, for example, that your partner and you were both very fit. Somewhere along the line, they gained weight while you have stayed fit. Now you are unhappy and unsatisfied with your partner. So how do you solve this? A long conversation about your feelings? Nope. Who has time for that? Just be straight forward and tell them, "You're fat. You need to lose twenty pounds" then change the topic drastically. It's that simple. The seed has been planted in their head.

You might be thinking, *Shit! That didn't sound offensive at all.* Or *Wow! You can't just say that. You're an asshole!* Just wait. It's going to make sense pretty soon. In the medical world, when you have patient that is in critical condition, we have to establish our baseline to determine how we are going to treat our patients. For instance, if we had a patient who died in a car wreck, they may or may not be conscious. They may be bleeding out or have internal bleeding. Maybe a few broken bones? We have to determine what is critical and what must be treated first.

This is the same concept we can apply to our relationships. If you have a partner who continues to break you down, in one or more ways, then you must establish which battle is important and which isn't. But hell, if you have only one issue, then this makes it a lot easier.

So here is your crash course in working on an ambulance. Everything is going well. Maybe you and your partner are having some lunch. Then boom. The car crash we spoke about earlier occurs. Let's say the patient is unconscious with minor bleeding and a broken leg. The main priority would be to open the airway and control respiration and then determine if CPR is needed. Cool. Your patient is breathing and has a pulse. Let's throw them on some 02 treatment as a precaution. He is just knocked out. The next step would be to control the bleeding. Great. Now splint the leg, backboard, and keep him warm while we transport.

These steps are the exact same you can do to establish a strong baseline for your relationship. Your partner is being distant, you're not having sex, and all you do is argue. Does this sound fucking familiar? Cool. We have all been there before. Now it's time to determine what you want and what's important. Sex and not fighting are your main priorities.

So now that we know what the issues are, we need to determine what is causing them. Why does your partner deny sex? What do they say or do every time you ask or make an effort? What triggers a fight? How often are you fighting? How are you responding?

We need to determine what the patterns are when these situations occur. You wouldn't start a mission without knowing exactly what you are getting into or at least have an idea. You prepare for the worst in battle. This is the same with your relationship.

# CASE STUDY 1

## Sergeant Jacobs

Sergeant Jacobs was assigned to the field for his duty weekend. He was constantly stressed out due to his wife. Finally in the field, he opened up about his relationship's problems. She was bitching every day about his career in the military and was tired of him always being away from the family. His wife had transitioned from phase 1 to phase 2 military spouse. Please note that in phase 1, the spouse is supportive almost like a cheerleader.

As the day in the field continued, he continued to bitch about his wife until he was finally told the truth about wine them, dine them, then deny them. As most individuals are told this method, he was in denial. He continued the road he was on.

Weeks later, he didn't go to the field. Sergeant Jacobs was standing duty for the barracks. He got fucked like most of us do and was called in. As most of us can figure it out, his wife was beyond pissed off because they had planned that weekend. Sergeant Jacobs was pissed because now he was involved in a three-way that wasn't a blessing.

At this point, he was desperate for change. Sergeant Jacobs was reminded of our method once again. He decided it was time to give it a chance. That week he went home and verbally let her have it. No filter. Over the next week, his wife absorbed the information and did not make any changes. (We have to be prepared for this.) Rather than continuing the process, he continued to wine her up without denying her. He gave in. Sergeant Jacobs went back to being a bitch.

- Miscommunication occurred when he failed to continue the process.

CHAPTER

$$\boxed{3}$$

# Making The Process Work for You

Now you may be telling yourself, "OK, I know what pisses me off with him [or her]. I know what triggers his [or her] emotions." Good. Keep that in the back of your mind because the real question is "How are you responding to your partner?" Are you giving in to their demands in order to save the relationship? Are you showing a lack of confidence in yourself, or do continue to hold yourself high?

You don't have to answer that question out loud. Better yet, answer it out loud. Don't hide behind your response or lack of response. There is no making excuses for your actions in the past. They are simply stepping-stones to a better you. Take every interaction with your partner as a learning experience.

When you first started dating your partner, you learned what their likes and dislikes were. This is constantly changing. Most people failed to continue to learn their partner. We start out at a high school level but never continue to earn our college degree. This takes a lot of work. But in reality, we are not just learning about our partners. We have to learn about our own actions and decisions.

Every action has a reaction. With this being said, your partner has learned how to take advantage of your wants and needs. If you partner knows that you are afraid to lose them, they will use that as leverage to convince you to give into their side. They will deny you of sexual gratification.

So again, ask yourself this simple question: "How do you respond to your partner when they fight with you?" Well, there is no simple answer. However, there is a way to break this spell that they cast over you. You must develop your own confidence in yourself and not just give in.

Again, sounds simple, right? Truth be told, if you can flip the switch on what they use as leverage on you, their attitude will change. However, the key is being consistent and not just giving in to your partner. Continue to have confidence without making it obvious that you are doing this.

So you may be wondering, *How do I do this? We already are at a rocky point.* Again, you don't need a PhD to fix your relationship. It's simple. Let's use sex as our example. Your partner has been denying you of sex because they know it will cause you to break down and fall into whatever they desire.

The first step is simple! Don't let it fucking bother you! Just go with the flow. I promise they will go to bed mad or at least act like they are made. Continue to do this for a little while. It will start to get the mind spinning. Continue to stick to what you said. Remember having balls means acting like a fucking man. Just keep in mind we are not saying treat your partner like shit. Just show some authority.

The second step is to buy her flowers or take her out to a nice dinner. Treat him or her with respect. However, here is the key: do not have sex with your partner. I repeat: do not have sex! Go out to dinner, make them laugh, and show them the new you. Hell, you can even rub their back in bed that night. But do not fuck them!

Right now, you are regaining attraction in your partner's eyes. There has been nothing but distance between you two for a while. Everything you have done to this point has done nothing but caused more stress or fighting because in their eyes, you are the bad guy. So with some distance from fighting and from reattracting, you will begin to see a shift in their behavior.

You might be saying to yourself, "Why wouldn't I want to fuck my partner? I love them, right?" Here is the simple truth: you are now gaining control over the situation because you are now denying them of what they hold over your head. You have taken away the ammo that they have been loading while waiting for their next time to strike.

Again, this isn't a simple task, and it's going to have to be done more than one night in order to allow your partner to begin to realize their tactics aren't working. Over time, they will begin to break down, and new habits will form—habits that will be more beneficial for you.

Keynote

1. This only works if you are good at sex. If you suck in bed, then I suggest watching some porn!

2. This process takes time. Don't lose hope.

3. If they start fucking someone else, then the process has also worked. Congratulations. You won! You can go fuck someone else who knows how to treat you right!

CHAPTER

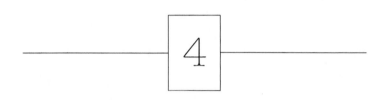

## Keep The Faith

As we said before, the easiest step is the initial step. Anyone can cook a nice dinner for your significant other. Anyone can clean up around the house or give their partner a nice massage after a hard day of work. The hard part is continuing to challenge you partner while they begin to constantly challenge the new you.

When you change your mindset from being the victim to being in control, you will naturally begin to regain your confidence. Your partner will feed off this and begin to challenge you. In every relationship, there is a fight for power. Each individual wants to express their point of view without judgment, be respected, and still have their self-worth. With this being said, we tend to pull the strings of our partner when we do not feel this way.

Similar to how we raise children, our actions and decisions affect how they respond. Take a young child who sees a toy in the window and starts crying that they want it. Do you just give in and buy the toy? Fuck no! You can't give in to negative fucking behavior; this reinforces the negative behavior by rewarding it. If you continue to feed this behavior, then they will know if they cry, you will give in because you don't want to deal with it.

Does this sound familiar? Good. It should. Again, we are going to be blunt with you. By continuing to allow your partner to disrespect you and by reinforcing their negative behavior, they will continue to learn that their behavior is acceptable. This of course means you will never be treated the way you wanted.

By establishing your baseline, you will begin to reestablish your dominance as well as your identity. Your partner will begin to recognize the difference. This is a good sign. They will realize there is a fucking problem because you won't fuck them. This will cause mental frustration for them as well as sexual frustration. Their minds will naturally circle back toward your last argument with them. This will cause them to question what the problem is due to them not having control.

In most cases, your partner will act out as the child in the store. They will get angry and continue to blame you. This is their attempt to make you feel shitty. But that's OK because you read this book so you know it's coming. After this is done and they see that their efforts are failing, they will start to bargain with you, trying to tell you what you want to hear. Again, don't give in; don't accept their offers. Otherwise, the cycle will continue. You might be asking yourself, "But isn't that what I wanted the whole time?"

Yes, it is, but it is not genuine. The cycle will continue to repeat itself. You need to rinse and repeat. They will treat you nicely, feed you up with positivity for one minute, and then belittle you the next. It will feel like an endless roller coaster. Stay strong; steady the course. You need to keep the faith and continue to trust the process. Continue to treat them with respect, but continue to respect yourself. Again, you did not do anything wrong except allowing the negative behavior to continue for so long.

# Case 2
## Kevin

Kevin decided to make a drastic decision when he didn't feel he was in control over his relationship anymore. He noticed that his wife at the time would use sex as a weapon to control the flow of the relationship. Kevin would agree because he wasn't going to cheat on his wife because that wasn't the man he was brought up to be. He was a family man who believed in his wife and kids. She had him in a psychological box. It fucking sucked.

So as time went on, one day Kevin decided he wasn't in the mood to fuck her. He said no, rolled over, and went to sleep. He didn't think anything of it. He repeated this several nights in a row. One morning she woke up earlier than Kevin. She had made breakfast for him—one of the things Kevin had complained about in the past.

Kevin found this change in her to be interesting. So once again, Kevin denied his wife of sex. The next morning, Kevin woke up to not just breakfast but breakfast in bed. She then blew him in bed, which he was OK with because he finally got his breakfast in bed. So the idea finally came to Kevin that denying sex can go both ways.

He then began to analyze what happened in more detail and created his own baseline. He realized his relationship sucked so he was going all in. Kevin decided to be bold. She was fat and had hygiene issues and issues with money. So one day when they had one of their normal arguments, Kevin laid into her. (Not the sexual way either.) Kevin told her she was fat and disgusting and he was sick and tired of her bullshit. She was an embarrassment in Kevin's eyes. He felt he had to babysit not just his own kids but hers as well. He told her it was time to unfuck herself or it was over. Mic dropped.

He then began the process of denying her. During this time, he never said why. He didn't repeat what he said after that night. Just continued to deny. He kept the same positive attitude.

Eventually one morning, she asked for help with managing her money. Kevin thought it was great. But he failed to continue to deny her. He slipped back in to having sex with her. Kevin realized he screwed up. He knew he was only human. So he began the process all over again. Eventually it started working. He continued the process, this time until he saw changes in all aspects he listed.

- Just because they do something nice doesn't mean you stop the process.
- Once you're in a position where you think they realize what's going on, give a little bit and wine them. (No sex.)
- You have control when you're able to deny them. Don't cheat. They will know and ruin the whole process.

CHAPTER

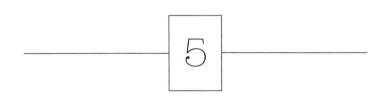

## Rinse and Repeat

So how will you know when this process has actually worked for you? When will you be able to tell when your partner actually wants only you? Where do we go from here? Sadly, there is no simple fucking answer, my friends. The real answer is simply a question for you to answer. Have you regained the ability to recognize your own self fucking worth? Or are you still being a pussy?

Again, we are just being honest with you; we can only set the guidelines. You have to be the one to follow the steps and commit to finding your equilibrium that was once lost. You have the ability to change your life, to improve how others view you, but more importantly how you view yourself. We can tell you how or what you need to do to be successful, but you have to be the one who wants to make the change and fucking do it.

Your partner will respond to your behavior and treat you accordingly. There will be times you will fight, there will be times you will want to give in, and there will be times when they will say shit that will be fucking hurtful. But stand your ground. Your will power and perseverance will get you through this internal hell.

Remember creating space and reattraction is key in order to calm their soul. (Insert *Mortal Kombat* voice.) This allows them to bring their guard down and allows them to see how you have changed. Again, not changing to fix the fight but changing to be a better person. It's about discipline and understanding. This is the key principle; you must constantly be repeating this step.

Now keep this in mind: You cannot keep using the same tactic every time. You have to adapt.

Just like in the field or when fighting a house fire, not every fire is the same. Not every fight is the same. Same goes for your relationship. With this being said, sometimes denying them sex is all that is needed. But the baseline has to be established first.

Regardless, you need to be in control. Most relationships are based upon emotions rather than logic. Now you have the ability to see this. Now it's your time to act and achieve your greatness. These strategies are based upon human nature and understanding the human fucking mind. Now go get your wife or partner back. Have crazy sex, and remember to rinse and repeat!

# CASE STUDY 3
## Firefighter Thomas

Firefighter Thomas was assigned to engine 2. Firefighter Smith had just finished his probationary period. He was spending money left and right. He met a girl he fell in love with. They partied hard every night. Firefighter Smith finally decided after one year of dating that he wanted to marry her. He finally dropped to one knee and popped the question. No surprise she said yes.

The problem was that the woman he wanted to marry was a stripper. Four nights out of the week, she was working in the club. He realized he didn't want a fucking stripper but a wife. So young Firefighter Thomas decided that he was going to give her a choice after talking to a senior firefighter who gave him some advice. She could either be his wife and find honest work or break up.

For three months, he did not attempt the process. His fiancée didn't make it easier with the consistent bitching. She made twice the money on the weekends as most did working full time. They began to fight more and more. Despite this, he continued to fuck her on a regular. He never denied her and fell into her web.

This continued three months after they were engaged. Finally, one night Firefighter Thomas had enough because the guys at work were busting his balls about marrying a stripper, he called her out. The problem was she decided that she wasn't going to change. Firefighter Thomas failed to follow the steps. He engaged her choices rather than sticking up for his beliefs.

- By not denying them of sex, your partner learns there are no consequences.
- You have to accept if they choose to leave.

# CLIFFS NOTES

- Grab your balls, and realize you're not to blame.
- Realize you have more control than you fucking realize.
- Reattract your partner.
- Deny them their main desire: sex.
- Continue to repeat while grabbing your balls; change your tactics of denial.
- Find the new you while your partner falls for you. Be the person you were meant to be!

# ADDITIONAL KEY TERMINOLOGY

- Phase 1 spouse: The spouse is pro military or pro first responder. They are your biggest fan. They want everyone to know that they are married to a hero. They may wear a shirt that says, "Army wife."

- Phase 2 spouse: They hate every aspect of the job. They hate the time you spend away from the family and continue to remind you every day.

- Phase 3 spouse: This is the middle ground between phase 1 and phase 2. They may hate that you are deployed or are away but understand this is a career. With this being said, they are more of a professional spouse. They understand your job sucks. They tend to not be jumping for joy or complaining in front of guests, but they might wear in public a pin that says, "The Key Wives Club" (aka "The Key Knives Club" and "Fucking Bitches.")

As always, stay classy, my friends. Don't drink responsibly, and enjoy your fucking life!

# ABOUT THE AUTHOR

## Deacon Frost

A proud American, husband, father, brother and veteran.

## Rip Matthews

An American contemporary writer, known for his informal and non-conformist literary style.

Printed in the United States
by Baker & Taylor Publisher Services